My World of Geography
RIVERS

Angela Royston

www.heinemann.co.uk/library
Visit our website to find out more information about **Heinemann Library** books.

To order:
 Phone 44 (0) 1865 888066
 Send a fax to 44 (0) 1865 314091
 Visit the Heinemann Bookshop at www.heinemann.co.uk/library to browse our catalogue and order online.

First published in Great Britain by Heinemann Library, Halley Court, Jordan Hill, Oxford OX2 8EJ, part of Harcourt Education.
Heinemann is a registered trademark of Harcourt Education Ltd.

© Harcourt Education Ltd 2004
The moral right of the proprietor has been asserted.

Editorial: Andrew Farrow and Dan Nunn
Design: Ron Kamen and Celia Jones
Illustrations: Jo Brooker (p. 11), Jeff Edwards (p. 5, pp. 28–9)
Picture Research: Rebecca Sodergren, Melissa Allison and Debra Weatherley
Production: Duncan Gilbert

Originated by Ambassador Litho Ltd
Printed and bound in Hong Kong and China by South China Printing Co Ltd

The paper used to print this book comes from sustainable resources.

ISBN 0 431 11789 6
08 07 06 05 04
10 9 8 7 6 5 4 3 2 1

British Library Cataloguing in Publication Data

Royston, Angela
Rivers. – (My world of geography)
1. Rivers – Juvenile literature
I. Title
551.4'83

A full catalogue record for this book is available from the British Library.

Acknowledgements

The Publishers would like to thank the following for permission to reproduce photographs:

Alamy Images pp. **4** (Jacques Jangouse), **9** (Robert Harding P.L./T. Gervis), **24** (Adrian Arbib); Associated Press p. **13** (Pavel Rahman); Corbis pp. **7** (George Huey), **14** (Yann Arthus-Bertrand), **16** (Eye Ubiquitous/J. Waterlow), **19** (Kevin Schafer), **20** (Roman Soumar), **21** (Charles O'Rear), **22** (Yann Arthus-Bertrand), **23**; Corbis Sygma p. **6** (Caron Phillipe); Geoscience Features p. **25**; Getty Images/Photodisc pp. **18**, **26**, **27**; Harcourt Education Ltd p. **15**; London Aerial Photo Library p. **10**; Photo Library Wales p. **8** (David Williams); Science Photo Library pp. **12** (Martin Bond), **17** (Robert Brook).

Cover photograph reproduced with permission of Getty Images/Stone.

Every effort has been made to contact copyright holders of any material reproduced in this book. Any omissions will be rectified in subsequent printings if notice is given to the Publishers.

Contents

Some words are shown in bold, **like this**. You can find out what they mean by looking in the Glossary.

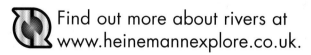 Find out more about rivers at www.heinemannexplore.co.uk.

What is a river?

A river is a large stream of water that flows across the land. It usually starts high on a mountain. It ends when it flows into the sea or a lake.

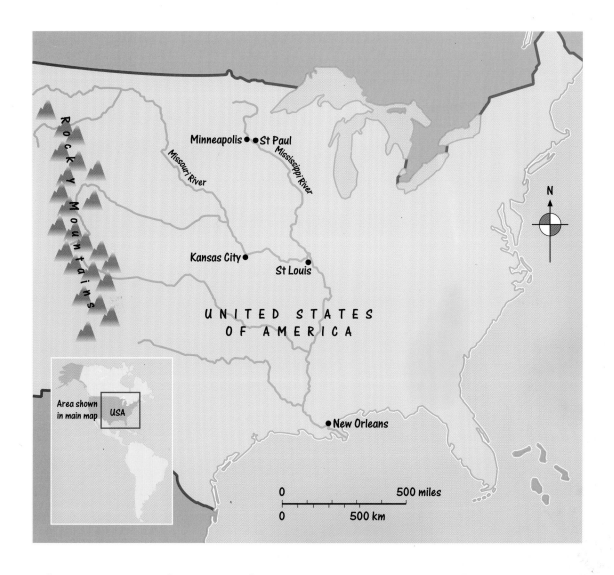

This map shows the rivers as wiggly blue lines. Rivers are always coloured blue on maps, even if they look brown in real life.

Where do rivers begin?

The **source** of a river is the place where it begins. Sometimes water flows from a hole in the ground called a **spring**. The spring water might even be hot!

The water in this hot spring spurts up from deep inside the Earth.

Water runs down a hill or mountain when it rains or when snow melts. The flowing water forms many tiny streams. Some streams join together to make a bigger stream.

River valleys

A stream flows down a hill or mountain to the **valley** below. As it flows along, it is joined by other streams. Soon the stream becomes a river.

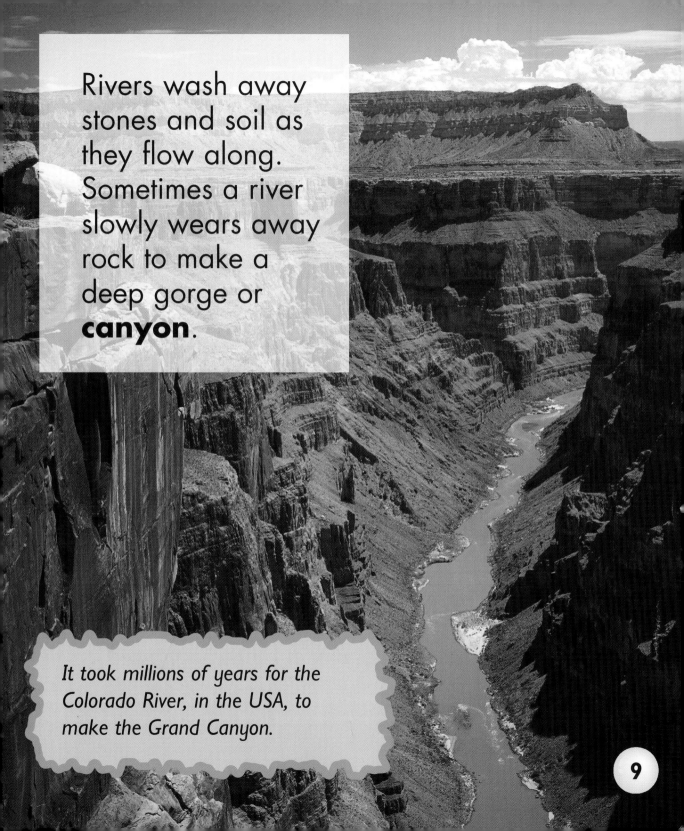

Rivers wash away
stones and soil as
they flow along.
Sometimes a river
slowly wears away
rock to make a
deep gorge or
canyon.

It took millions of years for the
Colorado River, in the USA, to
make the Grand Canyon.

Flowing over flat land

A river soon leaves the mountains and flows over flatter land. It becomes wider and the water flows more slowly. Sometimes a river flows around higher land and forms a large bend.

This river flows through the city of Durham, in the UK.

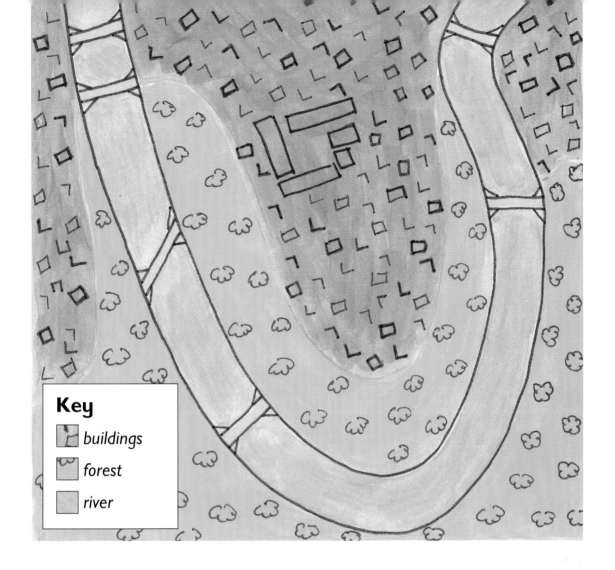

Key

buildings

forest

river

This map shows the same stretch of river as in the photograph. You can see how the river bends and where the bridges cross the river. You could draw a map like this.

Flooding

When snow melts in the mountains, more water flows into rivers. Rivers may become so full they **overflow**. Rivers may also overflow if it rains a lot.

Sometimes water breaks through the
banks of a river and covers the fields
near by. If there is a town or city near the
river, the water may **flood** the streets.

Reaching the sea

The **mouth** of a river is where the river flows into the sea. The fresh river water mixes with the salty sea water.

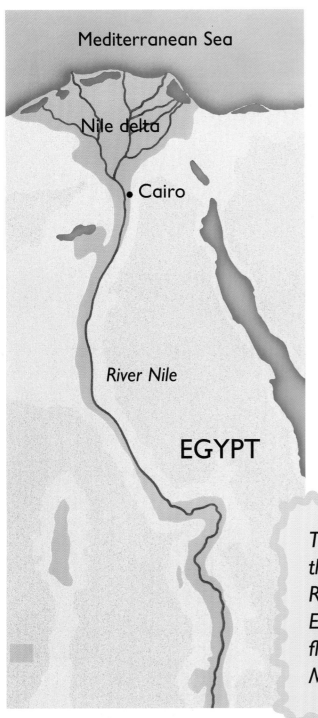

Mediterranean Sea

Nile delta

● Cairo

River Nile

EGYPT

A river is widest at its mouth. Sometimes the river mouth spreads out to make a triangle shape called a **delta**. Banks of mud form in the river's mouth.

This map shows the delta of the River Nile in Egypt. The Nile flows into the Mediterranean Sea.

Using river water

Farmers may use river water to water the fields near by. They dig ditches or use pipes to take the water from the river to the fields.

People use river water in factories and in homes. **Paper mills** use a lot of water. They are often built on the **banks** of a river.

Travelling by river

People use boats to travel along rivers. The boats take them from one town to another. In some countries, it is easier to travel by river than by road!

This boat is taking tourists on a river trip.

Where there is no bridge, people can use a boat or a **ferry** to cross the river. Ferries can carry people, cars, trucks or farm animals.

Carrying goods

River boats carry things, as well as people. In some places, farmers carry fruit and vegetables by boat to sell in the towns and cities.

These women are selling fruit and vegetables at a floating market in Thailand.

Trees are often taken down rivers to be made into **timber** and paper. The logs are pushed into the water and floated **downstream**. They do not need to be put on a boat.

Ports

Ports are towns where ships load and unload **goods**. Ships carry goods across the sea. Many ports are at the **mouth** of a river.

The port of Manaus in Brazil is hundreds of kilometres up the River Amazon.

Some ports are a long way up the river. Big ships can sail far up deep, wide rivers. Smaller boats take goods to ports up narrow or shallow rivers.

Rivers in danger

Rivers are easily harmed. If people take too much water from a river, the river dries up.

Many **factories** pour waste **chemicals** into rivers. Chemicals that farmers put on their fields are washed into rivers too. Some of these chemicals poison the water and kill the fish.

Enjoying rivers

Many people go to rivers for fun. Paddling a **canoe** through fast-flowing water is very exciting. Some slow, gentle rivers are good places to swim, but only if the water is clean.

Many people enjoy a quiet walk along the **banks** of a river. Fishing can be fun too. But it can be difficult to catch a fish in water that is moving quickly!

Rivers of the world

This map shows some of the biggest and longest rivers in the world.

Mackenzie

NORTH AMERICA

St Lawrence

Missouri

Colorado

Mississippi

Rio Grande

Amazon

SOUTH AMERICA

Mississippi-Missouri
Key fact: The Mississippi-Missouri is the longest river in North America.
Length: 6019 km (3740 miles)

Amazon
Key fact: The Amazon is the second longest river in the world.
Length: 6437 km (4000 miles)

 Find out more about rivers at www.heinemannexplore.co.uk

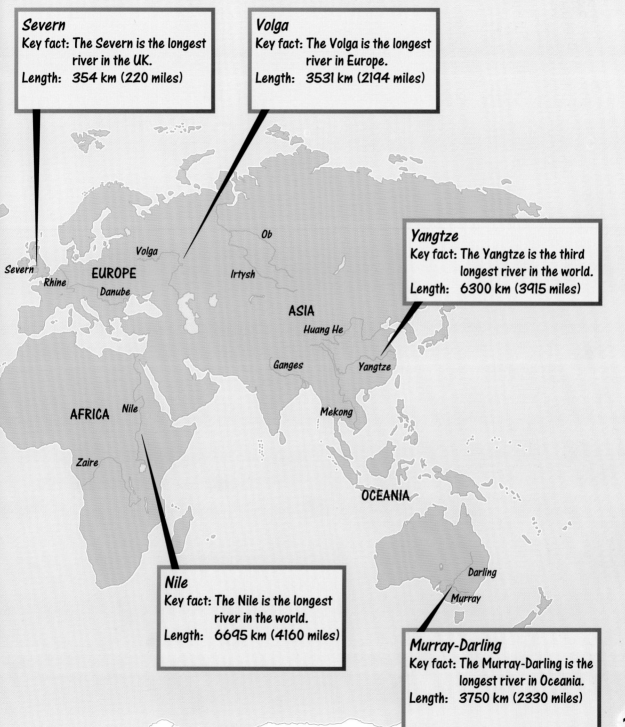

Severn
Key fact: The Severn is the longest river in the UK.
Length: 354 km (220 miles)

Volga
Key fact: The Volga is the longest river in Europe.
Length: 3531 km (2194 miles)

Yangtze
Key fact: The Yangtze is the third longest river in the world.
Length: 6300 km (3915 miles)

Nile
Key fact: The Nile is the longest river in the world.
Length: 6695 km (4160 miles)

Murray-Darling
Key fact: The Murray-Darling is the longest river in Oceania.
Length: 3750 km (2330 miles)

Ob

Volga

Severn

Rhine

EUROPE

Danube

Irtysh

ASIA

Huang He

Ganges

Yangtze

Mekong

AFRICA

Nile

Zaire

OCEANIA

Darling

Murray

ANTARCTICA

Glossary

bank the land along the edge of a river

canoe narrow boat that you move along using a paddle

canyon narrow valley with steep cliffs on each side

chemicals substances used by farmers and in factories

delta river mouth in the shape of a triangle

downstream the direction that a river flows in – this is always downhill

factory place where people make things

ferry boat used to carry people, cars and other vehicles

flood fill with water

goods things that are made, bought and sold

overflow spill over

mouth where a river meets the sea

paper mill factory that makes paper

port town or city where ships load and unload

source place where a river or stream begins

spring place where a stream of water bubbles up out of the ground

timber planks of wood cut from tree trunks

valley low land between two or more mountains

Find out more

Further reading

Geography First: Rivers by Nicola Edwards (Hodder Wayland, 2004)

Eye Wonder: Rivers and Lakes (Dorling Kindersley, 2003)

Geography Starts Here: Rivers and Streams by Jenny Vaughan (Hodder Wayland, 2001)

Make It Work! Geography: Rivers by Andrew Haslam (Two-can, 2000)

Geography Starts Here: Maps and Symbols by Angela Royston (Hodder Wayland, 2001)

Useful Websites

http://mbgnet.mobot.org/fresh/ – click on 'Rivers and Streams' for lots of information about rivers, including how streams become rivers, river animals and hydroelectric power.

www.teacherxpress.com/f.php?gid=25&id=4 – information from the BBC on rivers and how they are changing, particularly in Britain.

Disclaimer

All the Internet addresses (URLs) given in this book were valid at the time of going to press. However, due to the dynamic nature of the Internet, some addresses may have changed, or sites may have changed or ceased to exist since publication. While the author and the Publishers regret any inconvenience this may cause readers, no responsibility for any such changes can be accepted by either the author or the Publishers.

Index

Titles in the *My World of Geography* series include:

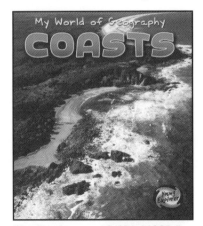

Hardback   0 431 11802 7

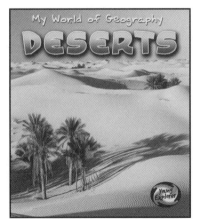

Hardback   0 431 11801 9

Hardback   0 431 11792 6

Hardback   0 431 11800 0

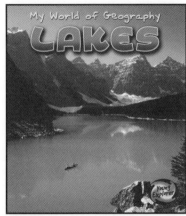

Hardback   0 431 11791 8

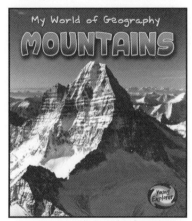

Hardback   0 431 11790 X

Hardback   0 431 11799 3

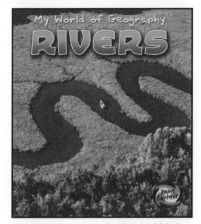

Hardback   0 431 11789 6

Find out about the other titles in this series on our website www.heinemann.co.uk/library